𝒴ellowstone is an ephemeral landscape, constantly shifting in response to natural processes. Its substance is rock, wood, bone, and sinew, but its essence is change. Sometimes suddenly, more often slowly and imperceptibly, forces shape the face of Yellowstone. Water, in manifold forms and subtle ways, is an instrument of change. Thrust to the sky in a superheated column, suspended in an evanescent mist, tumbling down to a distant sea, or trapped in a delicate crystalline snowflake, water alters the character of Yellowstone.

*T*he tiered and scalloped pools of
Minerva Terrace serve as a
colorfully evolving backdrop
to historic Fort Yellowstone.
The ledges are formed
of ornate travertine
deposits.

Yellowstone National Park, located in the northwestern corner of Wyoming, was the first national park. Established in 1872, it preserves unparalleled hydrothermal features.

Front cover: Old Faithful, photo by Larry Burton. Inside front cover: Bull elk in the Madison River, photo by Glenn Van Nimwegen. Page 1: Morning Falls, photo by Frank S. Balthis. Pages 2/3: Minerva Terrace, Mammoth Hot Springs, photo by George J. Schwartz. Pages 4/5: Yellowstone River, photo by Pat O'Hara.

Edited by Cheri C. Madison.
Book design by K. C. DenDooven.

Second printing, 1991
in pictures YELLOWSTONE The Continuing Story
© 1990 KC PUBLICATIONS, INC.

LC 90-60040. ISBN 0-88714-047-5.

in pictures
Yellowstone
The Continuing Story

By Sandra C. and
George B. Robinson

George Robinson is Chief of Interpretation at Yellowstone. During the last 29 years, he has served in similar capacities in several national parks, including Everglades and Wind Cave. His wife, Sandra, a teacher and former environmental education specialist, has authored three children's books and was a scriptwriter for a film about Yellowstone. The Robinsons have lived in Yellowstone National Park since 1982.

FRED HIRSCHMANN

*National park areas
are special landscapes set aside
by acts of Congress to protect
and preserve features of national
significance that are generally
categorized as scenic, scientific,
historical, and recreational.
As Americans, we are
joint caretakers of
these unique places,
and we gladly share them with
visitors from around the world.*

Yellowstone was once called "the place where Hell bubbled up." These words obscure the true character of this high, mountain-encircled plateau. They conjure up images of an inhospitable, perhaps lifeless, region. To the contrary, Yellowstone is animated, at once exciting and tranquil, a haven for wildlife and the human spirit. It is a place where we may discover and learn, a benchmark against which we may measure the tenor of our lives and times. The first of its kind, Yellowstone has been a model for the creation of parks all over the world.

This serene view of Mt. Washburn, shrouded in low clouds, belies its fiery past. Around 50 million years ago, it was an active volcano.

Earth, Fire, Water, and Air

The ancient landscape that was to become Yellowstone experienced repeated mountain-building episodes. Upthrust rock layers were folded, fractured, and altered by pressure and intense heat. Wind and water eroded the mountains down to a surface submerged beneath advancing inland seas. This period of sedimentation was followed by the uplift of the Rocky Mountains, and another cycle of volcanism, erosion, and deposition. More recentl in geologic time, the large centra. plateau was altered by the collapse, and subsequent refilling, of a huge caldera and by postvolcanic glaciation. Thus, Yellowstone was forged in a crucible of volcanic fire, tempered in glacial ice, and finely detailed by wind, water, and biochemical processes.

PAT O'HARA

The eroded ▷ north face of Bunsen Peak is a principal feature of the Golden Gate area. Thirty to fifty million years old, Bunsen Peak is part of an ancient volcano. The rock faces are golden due to the presence of yellow lichen.

▲ **The configuration of the land** and the vagaries of weather cause rain and melting snow to flow either to the Pacific or Atlantic oceans.

Relentlessly drawn downward by gravity, ▽ water seeks the lowest natural channels. Rivulets coalesce into streams; streams merge to become rivers. In the Absaroka Range, amid 50-million-year-old volcanic rocks, this timeless process gives birth to the Lamar River, one of many tributaries of the Yellowstone River.

At Sheepeater Cliff (right) and △ ▷
*Calcite Springs (above), basalt columns
formed when fine-grained black lava cooled
slowly and evenly. As the lava flow cooled, it
contracted and cracked into five-, six-, or
seven-sided vertical columns. The
"Sheepeaters" were the only resident group of
Indians in Yellowstone. Bighorn sheep
were their staple.*

RUSS FINLEY

△ **Unlike the Grand Canyon of Arizona, formed principally by the cutting action of the**
Colorado River, the Grand Canyon of the Yellowstone is the product of a coalition of forces: episodes
of filling from volcanic eruptions, glacial ice and floods, hydrothermal decomposition of rocks,
and the erosive action of wind, rain, and the Yellowstone River.

E*ach droplet a tiny prism, the mist rising from Tower Fall captures the sunlight* ▷
and transforms it into a beautiful rainbow. The waterfall, 132 feet high, was named for the
rocky "towers and pinnacles" which surround it. Visitors may follow a steep
half-mile trail to the base of the fall.

A Primal Force

Whether flowing, ▷ or in the form of snow, ice, or steam, water is a major erosive agent shaping the Yellowstone landscape. These snow-covered rocky spires in the canyon area are an example of hoodoo weathering and erosion.

◁ **F**rom the high Yellowstone plateau, rivers and streams course to the sea. Conforming to the variable topography created by lava flows, glaciers, and their own erosive action, streams and rivers plunge over ledges to create spectacular waterfalls. Kepler Cascades follows the "steps" of the Firehole River.

The Yellowstone River ▽ is the last, great, undammed river in the lower 48 states. It originates southeast of the park in the Absaroka Range and eventually empties into the Missouri River.

FRED HIRSCHMANN

TOM ALGIRE

Of Water, Heat, and Rock

The geyser suddenly explodes with a roar. The waters that hang suspended for one shimmering moment may have last captured the sunlight when mountain man John Colter set his eyes on Yellowstone in 1807. The waters that issue from a geyser are "old." A drop of rain falling on Yellowstone travels a distance of one to two miles into the subterranean labyrinth. By the time it returns to the surface, hundreds—maybe thousands—of years have passed. A geyser has three main components: an ample water supply, an underground heat source, and a subterranean reservoir and network of cracks and channels. Rain and snow provide the first element. Molten rock, closer to the surface in Yellowstone than in other parts of the world, heats the rock with which the seeping water comes into contact. The heated water rises and eventually flows into the geyser's "plumbing system," which usually lies within 100 feet of the surface. This interconnected system, unique to each geyser, shapes its appearance and behavior.

◁ △ *Winter or summer, night or day, unseen or witnessed by hundreds of visitors, Old Faithful has erupted over 1 million times since its discovery. Members of the Washburn-Langford Expedition first officially recognized the geyser in 1870. After observing it for two days, they named it "Old Faithful" because of its predictability. Since its naming, a common misconception has been perpetuated.* You cannot set your watch by it! *The interval between eruptions has varied from 30 to 120 minutes. Rangers can predict the time of the next eruption only by recording the duration of the last. Will Old Faithful ever stop erupting? Geologic systems are not static; hydrothermal activity is dependent upon forces acting deep within the earth. After major earthquakes, such as the 1959 Hebgen Lake earthquake, Old Faithful's average interval increased. Geyser activity can be altered or stopped by seismic events or natural deposition of sinter within the plumbing system. Sinter, a siliceous mineral, is precipitated not only at the surface, but can also grow within the underground channels of a geyser's system and cut off the flow of water. Man is not in control here. He can only observe and record—and hope that the awe and wonder which Old Faithful inspires will continue for a long time.*

A Gallery of Geysers

▲ **Reminded of the crumbling turrets of a** Middle Age castle, an explorer of the Washburn Expedition named this feature Castle Geyser. Although it is an ancient geyser, growing over thousands of years, Castle is still active.

◀ **Steamboat, the tallest geyser in the world,** explodes to a height two or three times that of Old Faithful. The water phase lasting for 3 to 20 minutes is followed by the steam event (pictured) of 12 to 24 hours. Steamboat erupts in intervals of 4 days to 50 years.

JENNIFER WHIPPLE

RUSS FINLEY

▲ **Great Fountain Geyser** erupts as the sun sets over the Lower Geyser Basin. Early adventurers wrote that they spontaneously threw their hats in the air and shouted at the sight of Great Fountain playing. Viewing this dynamic interaction of water, heat, pressure, and steam, one cannot help but share their enthusiasm.

Against a backdrop of ▷ grass and lodgepole pines, Riverside Geyser spouts from the bank of the Firehole River. Consistent in height and length of eruptions, Riverside has varied little since its discovery in 1871. Due to its predictability and pastoral setting, it is a popular geyser.

A Study in Contrasts

◀ **O**f the estimated 10,000 thermal features in Yellowstone, no two are exactly alike. These features include geysers, hot springs, fumaroles, and mud pots. Geysers erupt; hot springs, due to inadequate heat or cooling of their large surfaces, do not. Fumaroles result when there is heat, but insufficient water, all of which turns to steam. And a bubbling mud pot develops when there is an accumulation of hot clay from acid attacking rock and soil. In addition to physical variations (cone shape and size, force and height of eruption, and plume configuration), Beehive (foreground) differs from Old Faithful by being very unpredictable.

FRED HIRSCHMANN

JENNIFER WHIPPLE

JENNIFER WHIPPLE

◁ △ **E**ncircled by opalescent colonnades of ice, Porkchop Geyser dons its winter mantle. In summer, the ice castle no longer conceals the shape of its crater. Sunlight is dispersed in an arc of spectral colors seeming to emanate from within the earth. For many years, Porkchop erupted intermittently with only a slight surge that seldom emptied its pool. In early 1985 it began to "play" continuously from an empty crater. Its eruption was accompanied by a loud, jet-like roar. Porkchop Geyser can no longer be seen in these winter or summer moods. It destroyed itself in a sudden steam eruption on September 5, 1989. Perhaps no other feature speaks so eloquently of the constantly changing nature of Yellowstone.

A Host of Hot Springs

◁ *Elk cows and a calf rest on the travertine ledges of Opal Terrace. Throughout the year, elk are commonly seen in the Mammoth area. However, a safe distance should always be maintained as cows, particularly in spring, are defensive of their young.*

GLENN VAN NIMWEGEN

FRED HIRSCHMANN

◁ *In Mammoth, there are numerous hot springs, but no geysers. The water that emerges at Mammoth is not hot enough to produce geyser activity. However, terrace waters are not cool; the temperature of Minerva Spring is about 161°F. As the hot water percolates through the limestone substrate, calcium carbonate is dissolved. When the water surfaces, limestone precipitates out and is deposited as travertine. When underground channels are blocked by deposits, water is diverted to other outlets, and the building of a new terrace begins.*

Narrow Gauge ▷ *Spring is a complex feature that has many vents (one pictured). Narrow Gauge Terrace (not visible) was named for its resemblance to a railroad bed. The terrace is a fissure ridge that is often a destination for naturalist-guided walks.*

LARRY ULRICH

▲ **N**ew Highland Terrace typifies the erratic nature of hot springs. New Highland Spring began flowing in the early 1950s. As the hot water established channels in the forested area, trees were killed and buried. Denuded of needles, these conifers will continue to stand for years. The terraces are constantly changing in appearance. Hot springs develop different drainage patterns, and travertine is rapidly deposited—sometimes over 20 inches per year!

RUSS FINLEY

△ **The spectral hues of Grand Prismatic Spring can be fully appreciated in this aerial view. Early** trapper Osborne Russell described it in his journal as a " boiling lake." Located in the Midway Geyser Basin, it is Yellowstone's largest hot spring.

The ▷ decorative scalloped edge and shape of this feature suggest its name—Punch Bowl Spring. Part of the "Daisy Group" in the Upper Geyser Basin, this spring flows continuously. Shrouded in steam, hot water bubbles quietly at its center.

RAY ATKESON

◁ *A fumarole* (or steam vent) releases only water vapor and hot gasses such as carbon dioxide and hydrogen sulfide. This fumarole is located in the Steamboat Point area on the shore of Yellowstone Lake. The snow-capped peaks in the background are part of the Red Mountains.

FRED HIRSCHMANN

◁ *Runoff channels meandering* from hot springs support a variety of organisms. Near the source, channel bottoms are white. As water flows from its origin, it cools; rivulets become colored. Hues range from light yellow to orange and, farther downstream, dark green. These colors primarily result from the presence of bacteria and algae. Bacteria can survive at temperatures exceeding 167°F (the upper limit for algae). Boiling pools and the seemingly sterile, white surfaces of the drainways support bacteria. Bacteria and algal mats form the base of the food chain in thermal areas.

Overleaf: At the Lower Falls ▷ the Yellowstone River plunges 308 feet, then flows through the Grand Canyon of the Yellowstone. Photo by Gary Ladd.

Of Antler, Horn, and Claw

▲ **C**overing more than 100 square miles a season, mature grizzly bears have tremendous habitat requirements. Unaware of political boundaries, the grizzly often ranges beyond the park's protection. The long-term survival of the great bear is dependent upon the cooperation of federal, state, and private landowners in maintaining the integrity of the Greater Yellowstone Ecosystem.

FRED HIRSCHMANN

GLENN VAN NIMWEGEN

▲ **R**ugged mountain terrain provides a safe haven for the bighorn sheep. Special adaptations of the hoof and the bighorn's musculature make it possible for the animal to negotiate precipitous heights.

◄ **G**enerally preferring the "solitary life," bull moose frequent wet habitats. Most active at twilight and sunrise, moose may often be viewed at Willow Park.

◁ **L**azily basking on warm rocks is a favorite activity of the yellow-bellied marmot. Nicknamed the "rockchuck," marmots prefer the security afforded by rocky habitats such as Sheepeater Cliff.

DIANA STRATTON

Intelligent and ▷ inquisitive, the river otter inhabits riparian environments. The otter's chocolate brown fur insulates it against the icy waters of Yellowstone.

JOHN P. GEORGE

◁ **T**he night chorus of a gray wolf pack has not been heard in Yellowstone since the early part of this century. Options are currently being examined for restoring this historically persecuted and misunderstood predator.

LARRY BURTON

Six species of snakes have been ▷ identified in the park. Only the prairie rattlesnake is poisonous, and it is generally found at lower, drier elevations north of Mammoth.

JENNIFER WHIPPLE

Of Tooth and Scale

Although coyotes are ▷
opportunists—feeding on almost anything—their most common food in summer and fall is voles and pocket gophers. Called "Song Dog" by Native Americans, the coyote is the subject of many Indian legends.

LARRY BURTON

DIANA STRATTON

◁ **S**ecretive by nature, badgers are most often identified by what they leave behind, their burrows. With their long, curved claws, badgers are well equipped for digging. Fierce and persistent, they hunt small mammals by excavating their tunnels. Badgers and coyotes sometimes "shadow" one another. Each is hoping the other will scare a rodent in its direction.

Beaver dams are ▷
fairly common, though the beaver population has declined since the 1920s. The engineer's materials are simple: sturdy sticks, branches, and mud. Through their dam-building efforts, beavers effect positive changes in their environment. Their ponds provide valuable habitat for waterfowl, moose, trout, and other wildlife. By trapping water and increasing moisture levels, the beaver's activities enhance browse growth for ungulates.

JOSEF MUENCH

Of Feathers, Flight, and Hollow Bones

JOHNNY JOHNSON—DRK PHOTO

▲ **D**ue to severe spring weather, when bald eagles are nesting, the breeding population is low in Yellowstone. However, summer or winter, visitors have a fair chance of seeing this sovereign of the skies.

GLENN VAN NIMWEGEN

▲ **A** male blue grouse inflates his colorful neck sacs in this mating display. Balsamroot is in bloom for this spring ritual.

From a low hunting perch, the great gray ▷ owl "listens" for the rustling of voles in the grass. Dense pine forests and adjoining meadows conceal this elusive bird.

GLENN VAN NIMWEGEN

△ **Expressing displeasure,** the trumpeter swan extends and beats its wings when its territory is threatened. The swan population fluctuates within the park; with the seasonal arrival of migrants from the north, the birds are more easily observed in winter than summer. Although protected within Yellowstone, swans suffer lead poisoning and loss of habitat beyond its boundaries.

Spindle-legged killdeers ▷ summer in hydrothermal areas. Typically shorebirds, they do not build nests, but lay their eggs on the cool, pitted surfaces of thermal environments. Algal mats in runoff channels provide a supply of spiders and flies.

A Time of Fire

Absent for hundreds of years, large fires returned to the aging forests of Yellowstone in the summer of 1988. Driven by powerful and capricious winds and fed by desert-dry fuels, small fires quickly merged into larger ones which grew into giants. By summer's end, flames had touched, in some way, nearly 800,000 acres of the Yellowstone landscape. Fires of the size and intensity of those that burned in Yellowstone in 1988 have swept through the region many times. Since the retreat of glacial ice from the plateau, nearly 12,000 years ago, massive fires have periodically cleansed, invigorated, and diversified the forests of Yellowstone. Perhaps every 300 to 350 years, they will revisit the area again, and they may be dwarfed in magnitude by other natural events.

▽ *Winds of 50 to 70 mph pushed raging crown fires on "Black Saturday," August 20, 1988.*

△ **Small mammals, like the red squirrel, are more** vulnerable to predation because of reduced cover after fires. However, most populations are quickly restored.

...and Change

Landscapes are continually altered by a kaleidoscopic array of forces. Among the instruments of change are: weather, erosion, plant succession, glaciation, earthquakes, floods, human activities, and fire. Change is an immutable characteristic of the process we call nature. There is no beginning nor end to that process. One series of changes simply merges into another, often slowly and subtly, sometimes quickly and on a grand scale. Thus it was in Yellowstone in 1988. Fire has increased Yellowstone's biological diversity, strengthened its ecological associations, and enhanced its human values...Yellowstone has been enriched, not impoverished, by fire.

GLENN VAN NIMWEGEN

◁ **In the wraith-like** aftermath of fire, abundant life flowers on the forest floor. Burned trees will remain black for a few years. During this time sugars remaining under the bark attract insects. The songs of birds will reverberate among the conifer skeletons as insect-feeding animals are drawn to the area. Eventually, the bark will be shed, and the trees will appear gray. Fire-killed timber can remain standing for 20 to 40 years.

The Opening Act

Our lasting impressions of the world are mainly visual ones. We remember best and longest what we have seen. Yet, measured in the shortness of a human life, natural change is almost indiscernible. Because we are generally unaware of changes shaping and reshaping our environment, we tend to fix images in our mind's eye, to believe that the world about us should always look as it did when we first saw it. For many years, visitors saw a Yellowstone not obviously changed in character... like having a photo album filled with only 50- or 100-year-old pictures. In the years to come, changing images will be added to the Yellowstone album providing a more complete record of the growth of the forest family. In the decades prior to 1988, we witnessed the end of a long series of ecological changes. In a way, we saw only the final act of the play. Now, and in the future, visitors may see the curtain rise, and the opening act of another grand ecological drama.

The plants of ▷ Yellowstone have evolved with fire. Although plant parts above the ground may be charred, root systems remain mostly intact. In a year's time, the plants sprout with new stems and leaves. With reduced canopy cover and ash-enriched soils, the increased sunlight, water, and nutrients foster growth. The deep-pink blooms of fireweed and yellow groundsel confirm the promise of renewal.

◁ **This meadow** north of Mt. Washburn was blackened in the fall of 1988. The following spring it emerged a vivid green accented by colorful wildflowers. Note the spotty burn pattern and the untouched aspens in the foreground.

GLENN VAN NIMWEGEN

◁ **Possibly intensified** by the effects of fire, this fan-shaped debris flow would probably have occurred even if the fires had not. In the summer of 1989, a thunderstorm released an estimated 2 to 3 inches of rain in 30 minutes. On this steep hillside, the ground could not absorb the water. The downwash was channeled into existing gullies and carried with it accumulated sand. In other areas of the park, mud slides swept cars off roadways.

RUSS FINLEY

△ **Astride the Continental Divide, the waters of Isa Lake support a luxuriant growth of pond** lilies. Attached by root stalks to the pond bottom, the leaves and flowers create cover for pond inhabitants.

DIANA STRATTON

LARRY BURTON

△ **The blossom of the** American pasqueflower heralds spring at the lower elevations.

◁ **A welcome sight in late May is the** profuse blooming of the monkey flower. In winter, taking advantage of spring-like conditions along thermal drainways, this plant grows close to the ground.

JENNIFER WHIPPLE

Season of Renewal

As the rhythms of nature ebb and flow with the transit of the earth about the sun, winter brings heavy blankets of snow and ice, piercing winds, and plummeting temperatures. It is often a time of stress, hardship, and death. The life of Yellowstone is tested for several harsh months each year, but winter eventually blends into the lengthening days and warmth of spring. Spring is the animator of Yellowstone. It is a season of birth and renewal.

◀ **A**bove 7,500 feet the retreat of snow banks *is accompanied by the advance of glacier lilies. Their sunny, upturned petals hang from abruptly recurved stems.*

*F*ollowing the ▷ *sweet, but brief days of spring and summer, cottonwoods along the Gardner River are clothed in fall foliage. The water level is low not only because of the season, but also because of drought conditions that have existed in Yellowstone for the past several years.*

GLENN VAN NIMWEGEN

ERWIN & PEGGY BAUER

▲ *In Yellowstone's early days, a six-day grand tour of the park by stagecoach cost $50. Today you can recapture the spirit of the Old West by taking a 30-minute stagecoach ride from Roosevelt Lodge.*

The People, For Their Benefit

Over 2.5 million people travel from all over the world to visit Yellowstone every year. It is the mother of parks—a uniquely American contribution to world culture. "Yellowstone" can be a mad dash to see Old Faithful erupt, a rigorous backcountry hike or ski trip, a contemplative stroll on boardwalks in a thermal basin, or a ranger talk by a crackling campfire—there is something for everyone. However, if the mother park is to remain our legacy for the future, then journeyers here must remember that they are only "visitors." They must respect the needs of wild creatures for whom Yellowstone is "home."

By "translating" the ▷ language of nature into the language of man, park ranger/ interpreters help visitors to better understand and appreciate the subtle values and significance of Yellowstone. A diverse schedule of interpretive services, including guided walks, historic demonstrations, special children's events, and evening programs, makes it possible for visitors to participate in activities that match their interests and available time.

NPS PHOTO BY JIM PEACO

◄ *On* groomed roadways, snowmobiles enable visitors to explore the park's interior despite severe winter conditions. However, this season is a time of great stress for wildlife. Thoughtful travelers give animals the right-of-way and view them at a safe distance.

JAMES TALLON

◄ *The snowcoach is a* warmer alternative to snowmobiling. Snowcoaches originate from Mammoth Hot Springs and Old Faithful (where park lodging is available in winter), as well as from Flagg Ranch and West Yellowstone. As Yellowstone rests, the slowed pace allows visitors a more intimate experience with a snow-shrouded wonderland.

Boating ▷ enthusiasts can gain access to Yellowstone Lake from the Bridge Bay Marina. Deceptively calm, Yellowstone's frigid waters driven by summer squalls can become dangerously turbulent.

DIANA STRATTON

...and Enjoyment

MARK E. GIBSON

◁ **Led by** knowledgeable wranglers, one- and two-hour horseback trips are offered by the park concessioner at Mammoth, Canyon, and Roosevelt Lodge. As the horses are gentle and trailwise, even the novice can experience the park as many of its earliest explorers and visitors did.

JAMES TALLON

◁ **Avid** fishermen travel from all over the world to test their skills in the park's blue-ribbon trout streams.

◁ **A prudent hiker** exercises caution while crossing a stream bottom cobbled with slippery algae-covered rocks. With over a thousand miles of trails, varying in degree of difficulty, Yellowstone is a mecca for hikers. Weather, terrain, elevation, mileage, and bear closures are factors to be considered before undertaking any backcountry trip. Check with the local ranger's station.

With the play of ▷ light and shadow on its tinted walls, the Grand Canyon of the Yellowstone has always defied the artist to capture its many moods. One of the first to try was Thomas Moran, who humbly acknowledged that the colors of the canyon "were beyond the reach of human art." At Artist Point, this painter accepts the challenge.

RAY ATKESON

◁ *Yellowstone National Park is an ideal outdoor laboratory in which to conduct research. A resident staff of scientists and technicians, augmented by independent researchers from colleges and universities, conducts a broad range of studies designed to garner knowledge fundamental to the preservation, management, and interpretation of park resources. In most years as many as 200 projects are underway. They cover a broad spectrum of interests including geyser monitoring, studies of uplift in the Yellowstone caldera, radio tracking of bears, the life history of lake trout, and the long-term effects of fire.*

JENNIFER WHIPPLE

Yellowstone Association

The Yellowstone Association assists in providing visitors with information about Yellowstone and its surrounding ecosystem. A non-profit organization founded in 1933, the association uses proceeds from sales of educational materials in park visitor centers to help fund projects ranging from training for Yellowstone's naturalist staff to self-guiding trail leaflets for many park areas. In addition, the association sponsors the Yellowstone Institute, which annually offers visitors over 80 field courses and seminars.

SUGGESTED READING

CRANDALL, HUGH. *Yellowstone: The Story Behind the Scenery.* Las Vegas, Nevada: KC Publications, Inc., 1977.

DE GOLIA, JACK. *Fire: The Story Behind a Force of Nature.* Las Vegas, Nevada: KC Publications, Inc., 1989.

MCENEANEY, TERRY. *Birds of Yellowstone.* Boulder, Colorado: Roberts Rinehart, Inc. Publishers, 1988.

ROBINSON, SANDRA C. (for young people) *Expedition Yellowstone, a Mountain Adventure.* Boulder, Colorado: Roberts Rinehart, Inc. Publishers, 1986.

STREUBEL, DONALD. *Small Mammals of the Yellowstone Ecosystem.* Boulder, Colorado: Roberts Rinehart, Inc. Publishers, 1989.

WHITTLESEY, LEE H. *Yellowstone Place Names.* Helena, Montana: Montana Historical Society Press, 1988.

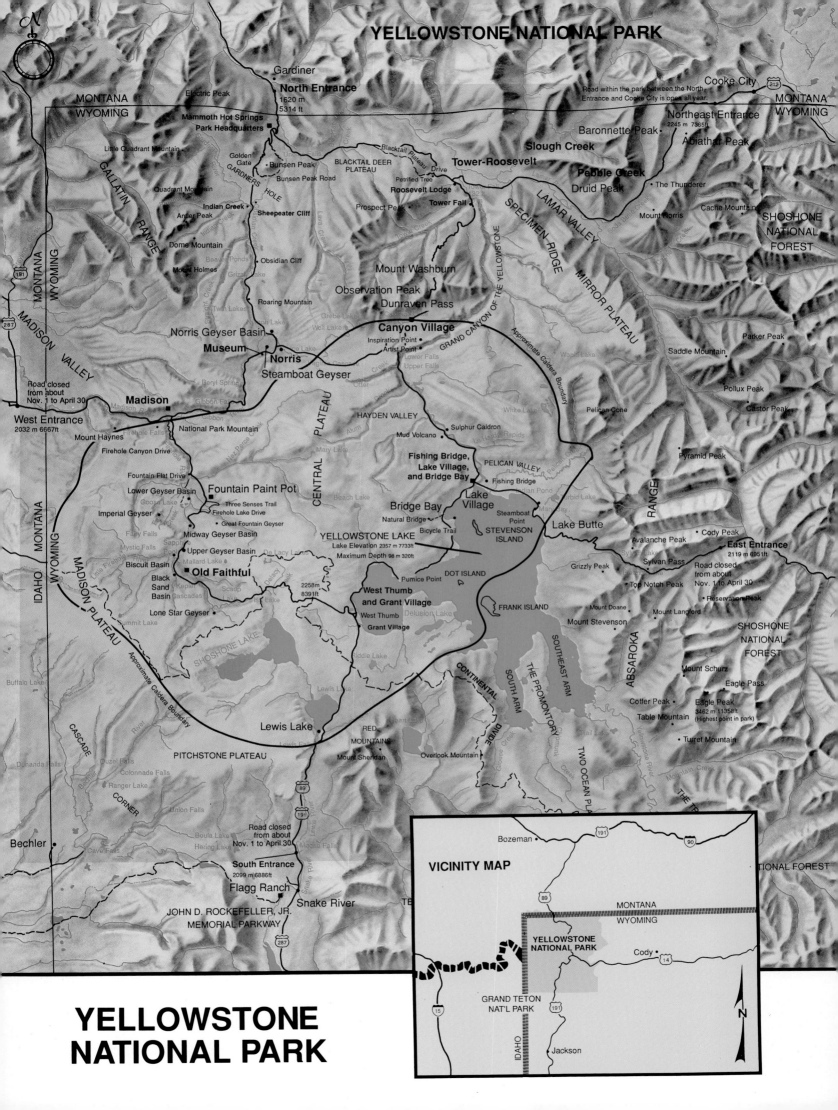

YELLOWSTONE NATIONAL PARK

YELLOWSTONE NATIONAL PARK

N

Gardiner •
Electric Peak •
North Entrance
1620 m
5314 ft

MONTANA
WYOMING

Road within the park between the North
Entrance and Cooke City is open all year.

Cooke City
212

MONTANA
WYOMING

Mammoth Hot Springs
Park Headquarters

Northeast Entrance
2245 m 7365ft

Little Quadrant Mountain •

Golden
Gate

• Bunsen Peak

Bunsen Peak Road

BLACKTAIL DEER
PLATEAU

Blacktail Plateau Drive

Tower-Roosevelt

Baronnette Peak •

Abiathar Peak •

Slough Creek

GALLATIN RANGE

GARDNERS HOLE

Petrified Tree

Roosevelt Lodge

Pebble Creek

Druid Peak

• The Thunderer

Quadrant Mountain •

• Indian Creek

Sheepeater Cliff

Prospect Peak •

Tower Fall

Mount Norris •

Antler Peak •

• Dome Mountain

• Obsidian Cliff

Beaver Ponds

Grizzly Lake

Mount Washburn

Cache Mountain •

SHOSHONE
NATIONAL
FOREST

Mount Holmes •

Roaring Mountain •

Observation Peak

LAMAR VALLEY

SPECIMEN RIDGE

Twin Lakes

Wolf Lake

Dunraven Pass

MIRROR PLATEAU

Norris Geyser Basin

Canyon Village

Grebe Lake

Inspiration Point

Parker Peak •

Museum

Norris

Ice Lake

Artist Point

Lower Falls

GRAND CANYON OF THE YELLOWSTONE

Saddle Mountain •

Steamboat Geyser

Upper Falls

Approximate Caldera Boundary

Wapiti Lake

Beryl Spring

Otter Creek

Pelican Cone •

Madison

Gibbon Falls

HAYDEN VALLEY

White Lake

Pollux Peak •

MADISON VALLEY

West Entrance
2032 m 6667ft

Gibbon River

Mud Volcano •

Sulphur Caldron •

Castor Peak •

Mount Haynes •

National Park Mountain •

NEZ PERCE

Firehole Canyon Drive

Alum Creek

La Hardys Rapids

Pyramid Peak •

Fountain Flat Drive

**Fishing Bridge,
Lake Village,
and Bridge Bay**

PELICAN VALLEY

Lower Geyser Basin

Fountain Paint Pot

Mary Lake

• Fishing Bridge

Indian Pond

Imperial Geyser •

Three Senses Trail

Firehole Lake Drive

• Great Fountain Geyser

CENTRAL PLATEAU

Beach Lake

Bridge Bay

**Lake
Village**

Mary Bay

RANGE

Fairy Falls

Midway Geyser Basin

Natural Bridge

Steamboat
Point
STEVENSON
ISLAND

Lake Butte

Mystic Falls

Sapphire Pool

Upper Geyser Basin

Bicycle Trail

Avalanche Peak •

• Cody Peak

Biscuit Basin

De Lacy Creek

YELLOWSTONE LAKE
Lake Elevation 2357 m 7733ft
Maximum Depth 98 m 320ft

East Entrance
2119 m 6951ft

**Black
Sand
Basin**

Old Faithful

Mallard Lake

Kepler Cascades

Pumice Point

DOT ISLAND

Grizzly Peak •

Sylvan Lake

Sylvan Pass

Road closed
from about
Nov. 1 to April 30

Lone Star Geyser •

Scaup Lake

2258m
8391ft

Isa Lake

**West Thumb
and Grant Village**

FRANK ISLAND

Mount Doane •

Top Notch Peak •

• Reservation Peak

Summit Lake

West Thumb

Grant Village

Delusion Lake

Mount Stevenson •

Mount Langford •

SHOSHONE NATIONAL FOREST

SHOSHONE LAKE

Riddle Lake

ABSAROKA

Mount Schurz •

CASCADE CORNER

Approximate Caldera Boundary

MADISON PLATEAU

Lewis Lake

RED MOUNTAINS

CONTINENTAL DIVIDE

SOUTH ARM

SOUTHEAST ARM

THE PROMONTORY

Eagle Pass

Coffer Peak •

Table Mountain •

Eagle Peak
3462 m 11358ft
(Highest point in park)

Buffalo Lake •

IDAHO
WYOMING

IDAHO
MONTANA

Ouzel Falls

Colonnade Falls

Ranger Lake •

Lewis Lake

Lewis Falls

Mount Sheridan •

Overlook Mountain •

Grouse Creek

TWO OCEAN PLATEAU

• Turret Mountain

Dunanda Falls •

PITCHSTONE PLATEAU

Bechler •

Beula Lake

Hering Lake

Union Falls

Lewis River

Moose Falls

Road closed
from about
Nov. 1 to April 30

Yellowstone River

THE TR

South Entrance
2099 m 6886ft

89
191

Flagg Ranch

Snake River

Cave Falls

Bechler River

JOHN D. ROCKEFELLER, JR.
MEMORIAL PARKWAY

287

VICINITY MAP

Bozeman •

191

90

89

MONTANA
WYOMING

**YELLOWSTONE
NATIONAL PARK**

Cody •

14

15

191

GRAND TETON
NAT'L PARK

NATIONAL FOREST

IDAHO

Jackson •

N

MONSERRATE J. SCHWARTZ

The national park idea, conceived here over a century ago, has passed from generation to generation, from continent to continent. It has been modified by time and place and circumstance. It has adapted to differing societies, cultures, and political ideologies, but it has endured the passage intact. Wherever it has spread from this magical place, it has enriched human life and experience. Many years ago, writer/interpreter Freeman Tilden said:

The early Greek philosophers looked at the world about them and decided that there were four elements: fire, air, water, and earth. But as they grew a little wiser, they perceived that there must be something else. These tangible elements did not comprise a principle: they merely revealed that somewhere else, if they could find it, there was a soul of things—a fifth essence, pure, eternal, and inclusive.

Yellowstone National Park is a place where we can all discover the "soul of things."

The heated waters from geysers and hot springs flow into the Firehole River on its journey north.

47

GLENN VAN NIMWEGEN

▲ *On March 1, 1872, President Ulysses S. Grant signed into law the Yellowstone National Park Act, creating the first national park in the world. Yellowstone thus was "...reserved and withdrawn from settlement, occupancy, or sale...and dedicated and set apart as a public park...for the benefit and enjoyment of the people...."*

Inside back cover: May the sun ▷ rise forever on the Yellowstone as man first saw it. Photo by Glenn Van Nimwegen.

Back cover: The free-roaming ▷ bison of Yellowstone embodies the spirit of wilderness we hope to preserve. Photo by Fred Hirschmann.

Published by KC Publications • Box 14447 • Las Vegas, NV 89114

Printed by Dong-A Printing and Publishing, Seoul, Korea
Color Separations by Kedia/Kwangyangsa Co., Ltd.